How To Play The Jew's Har

Step By Step Instructions To Play Songs

Copyright@2023

Raleigh Marion

Table Of Content

Introduction

A. Brief History And Cultural Significance Of The Jew's Harp

The Jew's harp, also known as the jaw harp, mouth harp, or Jew's harp, is an ancient musical instrument with a rich history and cultural significance across various civilizations. In this section, we will explore the instrument's origins, its cultural associations, and its journey through time.

1. Ancient Origins:

- Tracing back to ancient times: The Jew's harp has a history that stretches back thousands of years. The exact origin of the instrument is difficult to determine, but it is believed to have originated in Asia or Europe.

- Early archaeological evidence: The instrument's presence can be found in ancient civilizations such as China, India, Egypt, and the Roman Empire.

2. Cultural Significance:
- Shamanic and Ritualistic Use: The Jew's harp often held spiritual significance in various cultures. It was used in shamanic rituals, healing ceremonies, and trance-inducing practices.
- Folk Traditions and Oral History: The Jew's harp played an essential role in folk traditions, storytelling, and passing down cultural heritage through generations. It accompanied songs, dances, and celebrations.
- Symbolism and Mythology: In some cultures, the Jew's harp held symbolic meanings associated with fertility, protection, or magical properties. It was

often associated with mythological figures or deities.

3. Global Spread:

- Silk Road Influence: The Jew's harp spread along the ancient Silk Road trade routes, as it was carried by merchants, travelers, and musicians. It found its way to different regions, blending with local musical traditions and evolving unique playing styles.
- European Influence: During the medieval and Renaissance periods, the Jew's harp gained popularity in Europe, where it was embraced in courtly and folk music traditions. It was featured in compositions by prominent composers such as Mozart and Beethoven.

4. Cultural Diversity:

- Regional Variations: The Jew's harp took on different shapes, sizes, and materials depending on the region. Each variant had its unique playing techniques and musical styles associated with it.

- Indigenous Cultures: Many indigenous communities around the world have preserved their distinctive Jew's harp traditions. Examples include the Yakut people in Siberia, the Saami people in northern Scandinavia, and various Native American tribes.

5. Contemporary Revival and Adaptations:

- Modern Usage: The Jew's harp has experienced a resurgence in recent years, with musicians exploring its versatility in different genres such as folk, world music, and even experimental or contemporary compositions.

- Cultural Exchange and Fusion: The Jew's harp has become an instrument of cultural exchange, as musicians from diverse backgrounds incorporate it into their music, blending traditional and contemporary elements.

Conclusively, the Jew's harp carries a deep historical and cultural significance, serving as a bridge between ancient traditions and modern musical expressions. Its enduring popularity and widespread use reflect its captivating sound and its ability to connect people across time and cultures.

B. Overview Of The Instrument's Anatomy And Playing Techniques

Anatomy of the Jew's Harp:

The Jew's harp is a small, handheld instrument consisting of a frame and a metal reed or tongue. Although designs may vary, the basic anatomy includes the following components:

1. Frame:
- Mouthpiece: The part held against the performer's teeth or lips, typically made of metal or wood, providing stability and control.
- Arm or Frame Wire: A curved wire that extends from the mouthpiece and holds the reed.

2. Reed or Tongue:

- Lamella: The flexible metal or bamboo tongue that vibrates to produce sound. It is attached to the arm or frame wire and serves as the instrument's vibrating element.

Playing Techniques:

Playing the Jew's harp requires a combination of mouth and hand techniques to produce sound and manipulate pitch. Here are some fundamental techniques:

1. Placing and Holding:

- Positioning the Jew's Harp: Hold the instrument against your front teeth or lips, resting the frame against the teeth or the mouth cavity.
- Stable Grip: Ensure a firm but comfortable grip, allowing for control and maneuverability.

2. Mouth Movement and Resonance:

- Jaw Movement: Control the position and movement of your jaw to alter the shape of your oral cavity. Experiment with opening and closing your mouth slightly to achieve different resonances and tonal qualities.

- Tongue Placement: Position your tongue against the roof of your mouth or vary its position to modify the sound produced.

3. Plucking Technique:

- Finger Placement: Use your dominant hand to pluck the reed. Position your finger close to the tip of the reed, applying gentle pressure without dampening its vibration.

- Plucking Motion: Pluck the reed by flicking or pulling it away from the frame wire. Aim for a clean and crisp plucking motion to produce a distinct sound.

4. Articulation and Expression:

- Vibrato: Create a vibrato effect by rapidly and subtly varying the pressure on the reed while plucking. This produces a wavering sound and adds expressiveness to your playing.
- Mouth Articulation: Experiment with different mouth shapes and techniques, such as tongue clicking or tongue-slapping, to achieve percussive effects or alter the timbre of the sound.

5. Manipulating Pitch and Overtones:

- Mouth Cavity Variation: Change the shape and size of your oral cavity to manipulate the pitch of the sound produced. Larger oral cavities generally produce lower pitches, while smaller cavities produce higher pitches.
- Overtones and Harmonics: Explore the instrument's ability to produce multiple

simultaneous tones by selectively amplifying specific overtones. This technique involves controlling the position of your tongue and adjusting the resonating chamber.

6. Rhythmic Patterns and Melodies:

- Explore rhythmic patterns and repetitive sequences of notes to create engaging rhythms and grooves.
- Practice scales, intervals, and melodic patterns to play melodies on the Jew's harp. Experiment with different finger techniques and mouth articulation to achieve desired musical phrases.

C. Benefits Of Learning To Play The Jew's Harp

Learning to play the Jew's harp offers several benefits that go beyond the joy of creating music. Here are some advantages of learning and playing the Jew's harp:

1. Musical Expression: Playing the Jew's harp allows you to express yourself through music. You can explore different tones, rhythms, and melodies, and use the instrument as a means of personal artistic expression.

2. Portability and Accessibility: The Jew's harp is a compact instrument that is easy to carry, making it ideal for travel or playing in various settings. Its accessibility and simplicity make it suitable for musicians of all ages and skill levels.

3. Improves Breath Control and Lung Capacity: Playing the Jew's harp requires controlling the flow of air through your mouth and manipulating your breath to produce different sounds. Regular practice can help develop breath control and increase lung capacity.

4. Enhances Coordination and Finger Dexterity: Manipulating the Jew's harp with your fingers while controlling the oral cavity and jaw movements requires coordination and dexterity. Consistent practice has the potential to enhance the synchronization between your hands and eyes, as well as refine your fine motor skills.

5. Relieves Stress and Promotes Relaxation: Engaging in playing music, even on a simple instrument like the Jew's harp, can have a calming and relaxing effect.

It can help reduce stress, promote mindfulness, and provide a creative outlet for emotional expression.

6. Cultivates Focus and Mindfulness:
When playing the Jew's harp, you need to concentrate on the instrument, the sounds produced, and the techniques employed. This focus on the present moment promotes mindfulness, helping to improve mental clarity and concentration.

7. Cultural Exploration and Connection:
The Jew's harp has a rich cultural history and is associated with various traditions around the world. Learning to play it can foster an appreciation for different cultures, their music, and their artistic expressions, promoting cross-cultural understanding.

8. Social Engagement and Collaboration:
Playing the Jew's harp can be a social
activity, allowing you to connect with other
musicians and share musical experiences. It
can lead to collaborations, jam sessions, or
participation in musical ensembles, fostering
a sense of community and shared creativity.

9. Cognitive Stimulation: Learning and
playing a musical instrument like the Jew's
harp can stimulate cognitive processes,
including memory, pattern recognition, and
problem-solving skills. It challenges the
brain in unique ways and promotes cognitive
flexibility.

**10. Personal Satisfaction and
Achievement:** Progressing in your Jew's
harp playing skills, mastering new
techniques, and creating music can provide a
sense of personal satisfaction and

achievement. It offers a continuous learning journey and a means of personal growth.

Chapter 1: Getting Started

1.1 Choosing The Right Jew's Harp:

A. Different Types And Materials Of Jew's Harps

The Jew's harp comes in various types and materials, each with its unique characteristics and sound qualities. Here are some common types and materials of Jew's harps:

1. Traditional Metal Jew's Harps:

- Brass: Brass Jew's harps are commonly found and known for their warm and mellow sound. They are durable and produce a rich resonance.

- Steel: Steel Jew's harps are often preferred for their bright and crisp sound. They offer excellent responsiveness and clarity.

2. Bamboo Jew's Harps:

- Bamboo: Bamboo Jew's harps are popular in Southeast Asia. They are made from bamboo reeds and offer a distinct natural resonance and warm tones.

3. Wooden Jew's Harps:

- Hardwoods: Jew's harps made from hardwoods such as maple, oak, or rosewood are known for their resonance and tonal depth. They often produce a mellower sound compared to metal variants.
- Softwoods: Softwood Jew's harps, like those made from cedar or pine, are lighter in weight and offer a brighter and more delicate sound.

4. Horn Jew's Harps:

- Animal Horns: Some Jew's harps are made from animal horns, such as buffalo or ram horns. These instruments often produce a unique and raw sound with a distinct timbre.

5. Plastic or Synthetic Jew's Harps:
- Synthetic materials: In addition to traditional materials, Jew's harps can be made from various synthetic materials, including plastics. These synthetic variants often provide durability, affordability, and a range of sound possibilities.

6. Experimental and Modern Jew's Harps:
- Alternative Materials: Some Jew's harp makers experiment with unconventional materials like glass, ceramics, or even 3D-printed materials. These unique variations can offer different sound textures and experimental possibilities.

B. Factors To Consider When Selecting Your Instrument

When selecting a Jew's harp, several factors should be considered to ensure you find an instrument that suits your needs and preferences. Here are a number of some relevant key factors to consider:

1. Sound Quality and Tone:

- Different Jew's harps produce varying tones and sound qualities. Consider the type of sound you prefer, whether it's warm and mellow, bright and crisp, or something in between. Experiment with different materials and designs to find the sound that resonates with you.

2. Skill Level and Playing Style:

- Beginners may find it helpful to start with a Jew's harp that is easier to play and produces clear tones. More experienced players may prefer instruments that offer greater control and a wider range of expression. Consider your skill level and the playing style you aim to achieve.

3. Comfort and Fit:

- The Jew's harp should feel comfortable and fit well in your mouth. Consider the size and shape of the mouthpiece and ensure it is suitable for your dental structure and playing technique. Experiment with different models to find one that feels comfortable and secure when held against your teeth or lips.

4. Durability and Construction:

- Consider the durability and construction of the Jew's harp. Depending on your needs, you may prefer an instrument that is sturdy and resilient, especially if you plan to travel or perform frequently. Evaluate the quality of materials and craftsmanship to ensure the instrument will withstand regular use.

5. Budget:

- Determine your budget range and look for Jew's harps within that range. Prices can vary depending on factors such as materials, craftsmanship, and brand reputation. Set a budget that suits your financial situation and expectations for quality.

6. Brand Reputation and Reviews:

- Research and read reviews about different brands and models of Jew's harps. Look for reputable manufacturers known for producing high-quality instruments. Customer reviews can provide valuable insights into the instrument's sound, durability, and overall satisfaction.

7. Try Before Buying:

- Whenever possible, try out different Jew's harps before making a purchase. Play them to get a feel for the sound, playability, and comfort they offer. This hands-on experience will help you make an informed decision.

1.2 Proper Holding And Positioning:

A. Hand Placement And Grip For Optimal Control And Comfort

Hand placement and grip are essential for optimal control and comfort when playing the Jew's harp. Here are a number of some relevant tips to consider:

1. Hand Placement:

- Hold the Jew's harp with your non-dominant hand, while your dominant hand plucks the reed.
- Place the frame wire against the pads of your fingers, near the base of your thumb.
- Use the fingers of your non-dominant hand to support and stabilize the Jew's harp while playing.

2. Thumb Position:

- Rest your thumb lightly against the frame wire to provide stability and control. Avoid pressing too hard, as it may hinder the vibration of the reed.

3. Finger Position:

- Position your fingers on the frame wire to hold the Jew's harp securely but with a relaxed grip.
- Avoid gripping too tightly, as it can restrict the movement of the instrument and affect the sound quality.

4. Angling the Jew's Harp:

- Angle the Jew's harp slightly downward, away from your face, to allow for optimal mouth placement and prevent accidental contact with your teeth.

5. Comfort and Relaxation:

- Maintain a relaxed hand and arm position while playing. Tension can affect your control and impede your playing ability.
- If you feel any discomfort or strain, adjust your hand position or grip to find a more comfortable and natural posture.

6. Experiment and Adapt:

- Each individual may have slightly different hand sizes and finger lengths. Experiment with hand placement and grip to find what works best for you.
- Adapt your hand position as needed while exploring different playing techniques or musical passages to maintain control and comfort.

C. Correct Positioning Of The Jew's Harp Against The Teeth

Correct positioning of the Jew's harp against the teeth is crucial for achieving optimal sound production and control. Here are some guidelines to help you position the instrument correctly:

1. Mouth Cavity:

- Open your mouth slightly, creating a small cavity between your teeth and lips.
- Keep your tongue relaxed and resting on the bottom of your mouth.

2. Frame Placement:

- Hold the Jew's harp against your teeth, with the frame wire resting gently against the outer surface of your teeth or the inside of your lips.
- Ensure the frame wire is parallel to your teeth or slightly angled downward.

3. Stability and Control:

- Find a balance between a firm grip and maintaining a relaxed jaw and facial muscles.
- Use your non-dominant hand to stabilize the Jew's harp if needed.

4. Avoid Teeth Contact:

- Make sure the reed of the Jew's harp does not touch your teeth when plucked. The reed should vibrate freely without obstruction.
- If you find that the reed is hitting your teeth, adjust the positioning of the instrument by tilting it slightly or altering the angle of your jaw.

5. Comfort:

- Pay attention to any discomfort or pain while playing. If you experience discomfort in your teeth or jaw, adjust the positioning of the Jew's harp to alleviate any strain.

- Experiment with slight adjustments to find the most comfortable position that allows for clear sound production and ease of playing.

6. Individual Variation:
- Everyone's dental structure is unique, and the ideal positioning may vary slightly from person to person.
- Take some time to experiment and find the position that works best for you, considering factors like tooth alignment and mouth shape.

Chapter 2: Fundamental Techniques

2.1 Basic Mouth Movement:

A. Exploring Different Mouth Shapes And Techniques For Producing Sounds

Exploring different mouth shapes and techniques can greatly enhance your ability to produce various sounds and effects on the Jew's harp. Here are some mouth shapes and techniques you can experiment with:

1. Varying Jaw Position:

- Adjusting the position of your jaw can have a significant impact on the sound produced. Try opening or closing your mouth slightly to explore different resonances and tonal qualities.

2. Tongue Placement:

- Experiment with the placement of your tongue to alter the sound and timbre. Here are a few but vital techniques to try:

  - Tongue Against the Roof of the Mouth: Rest your tongue lightly against the roof of your mouth to produce a fuller and more resonant sound.

  - Tongue Away from the Roof of the Mouth: Keep your tongue relaxed and away from the roof of your mouth to create a brighter and sharper sound.

3. Articulation Techniques:

- Articulation techniques involve manipulating your tongue and mouth to produce percussive or expressive effects. Here are a few but vital techniques to explore:

  - Tongue Clicking: By quickly bringing your tongue into contact with the roof of your mouth, you can create a percussive clicking sound that adds rhythm and texture to your playing.

  - Tongue Slapping: Experiment with slapping your tongue against the roof of your mouth to create sharper percussive effects.

  - Tongue Fluttering: Fluttering your tongue against the roof of your mouth produces a rapid series of percussive sounds.

4. Mouth Resonance:

- Altering the shape and size of your oral cavity can modify the resonance and tone of the sound produced. Here are a number of few but vital techniques to try:

  - Wider Mouth: Open your mouth slightly wider to create a deeper and more resonant sound.

- Narrower Mouth: Close your mouth slightly to create a brighter and more focused sound.

- Shaping the Lips: Experiment with shaping your lips to create different sound effects. For example, rounding your lips can produce a more mellow and flute-like tone.

5. Vocalization:

- Combine the sounds produced by the Jew's harp with vocalizations to add depth and expressiveness to your playing. Experiment with humming, vocalizing vowel sounds, or even singing melodies while playing the instrument.

B. Exercises To Develop Mouth Control And Dexterity

Developing mouth control and dexterity is crucial for playing the Jew's harp with precision and finesse. Here are some exercises you can practice to improve your mouth control and dexterity:

1. Breath Control and Air Manipulation:

- Practice controlling the flow of air through your mouth by inhaling deeply and exhaling slowly and steadily. Focus on maintaining a consistent and controlled airflow while playing the Jew's harp.

- Experiment with varying the intensity and speed of your exhalation to produce different dynamics and nuances in your sound.

2. Articulation Exercises:

- Work on tongue articulation by performing tongue exercises like tongue rolls, flicks, and trills. These exercises help develop precision and control over tongue movements, which can be useful for producing percussive effects and nuanced articulations on the Jew's harp.

3. Jaw and Mouth Warm-Ups:

- Perform gentle jaw exercises by opening and closing your mouth slowly and smoothly. This helps relax the jaw muscles and prepares them for precise movements during playing.
- Stretch and relax your facial muscles by gently massaging your cheeks and jaw area. This promotes overall relaxation and flexibility in the mouth and face.

4. Tongue Placement and Movement:

- Practice moving your tongue to different positions within your mouth. Experiment with placing the tip of your tongue against the roof of your mouth, touching different teeth, or resting it at the bottom of your mouth.

- Try tongue exercises like moving your tongue from side to side or in circular motions. This helps improve tongue agility and coordination.

5. Lip and Jaw Control:

- Develop lip and jaw control by practicing lip trills and flutters. Gently vibrate your lips by blowing air through them while keeping them relaxed. This exercise improves lip flexibility and control, which are crucial for achieving different sounds on the Jew's harp.

- Practice opening and closing your mouth while maintaining a consistent sound on the

Jew's harp. This exercise helps develop independent control of your jaw movement and sound production.

6. Scale and Melodic Patterns:
- Play scales and melodic patterns on the Jew's harp to develop finger dexterity and coordination with mouth movements. Start with simple patterns and gradually increase the complexity as you improve.

7. Slow and Controlled Playing:
- Practice playing the Jew's harp slowly and with precision. Focus on maintaining a steady rhythm, clear articulation, and accurate pitch. This helps develop control and precision in your playing.

Remember to start with short practice sessions and gradually increase the duration as your mouth muscles become accustomed to the exercises. Regular practice and consistent effort are key to improving mouth control and dexterity. Over time, you will notice increased control, precision, and fluidity in your playing on the Jew's harp.

2.2 Mastering The Plucking Motion:

A. Techniques For Plucking The Jew's Harp With The Finger

Plucking the Jew's harp with your finger is a common technique that allows for direct control over the reed and can produce a wide range of sounds and effects. Here are some techniques to consider when plucking the Jew's harp with your finger:

1. Finger Placement:

- Use the pad of your index finger or middle finger to pluck the reed.
- Position your finger slightly behind the reed, closer to the frame wire, for better control and stability.

2. Plucking Motion:

- Use a quick, controlled motion to pluck the reed. The movement should be focused and precise, with the finger pulling the reed away from the frame wire and then releasing it.

3. Varying Finger Pressure:

- Experiment with the amount of pressure you apply with your finger. Lighter pressure can produce softer, more delicate sounds, while firmer pressure can create louder, more pronounced sounds.

4. Plucking Position:

- Explore different positions along the length of the reed to achieve various pitch and timbre variations. Plucking closer to the base of the reed generally produces lower pitches, while plucking closer to the tip produces higher pitches.

5. Combining Plucking and Breath:

- Coordinate the plucking motion with controlled exhalation to enhance the sound and expressiveness of the instrument. Experiment with different combinations of plucking and breath to create dynamic and nuanced effects.

6. Multiple Finger Techniques:

- Try using multiple fingers to pluck the Jew's harp simultaneously or in rapid succession. This technique can create complex rhythms and patterns, as well as produce richer and layered sounds.

7. Harmonic Overtones:

- Explore techniques for producing harmonic overtones by plucking the reed while subtly altering your mouth shape or tongue position. This can result in additional higher-pitched tones being produced along with the fundamental note.

8. Effects and Articulation:

- Experiment with different finger techniques to produce percussive effects or articulations, such as tapping the reed lightly with your finger or performing quick and controlled flicks on the reed.

B. Developing a Consistent And Precise Plucking Motion

Developing a consistent and precise plucking motion is essential for achieving control and accuracy when playing the Jew's harp. Outlined below are a number of some relevant tips to help you develop a reliable plucking technique:

1. Finger Position:

- Position your finger (index or middle finger) behind the reed, closer to the frame wire, for better leverage and control.
- Align your finger with the center of the reed, ensuring that it contacts the reed evenly.

2. Controlled Movement:

- Practice a controlled and deliberate plucking motion. Avoid excessive force or erratic movements that may cause the reed to vibrate inconsistently.

- Maintain a relaxed hand and finger position, allowing for fluid and controlled motions.

3. Consistent Contact:

- Ensure that your finger makes consistent contact with the reed each time you pluck. Inconsistent contact can result in variations in sound and disrupt your playing.

4. Plucking Speed:

- Experiment with different plucking speeds to find the optimal speed for the sound you wish to produce. Generally, a quick and snappy plucking motion yields clearer and more pronounced sounds.

5. Finger Strength and Dexterity:

- Strengthen your finger muscles through regular finger exercises and hand stretching exercises. This helps improve finger control and precision during plucking.
- Practice finger dexterity exercises, such as finger rolls or trills, to enhance your finger agility and coordination.

6. Metronome Practice:

- Utilize a metronome to practice maintaining a consistent rhythm and plucking motion. Start with a slow tempo and gradually increase the speed as you become more comfortable and accurate.

7. Recording and Self-Evaluation:

- Record yourself playing and listen back to assess the consistency and precision of your plucking motion. Pay attention to any variations or irregularities in the sound produced and identify areas for improvement.

8. Slow and Controlled Practice:
- Begin by practicing at a slower pace, focusing on maintaining a consistent and precise plucking motion. Gradually increase the tempo as you build confidence and accuracy.

9. Mindful Practice:
- Stay mindful and attentive to the plucking motion during your practice sessions. Avoid rushing or becoming complacent. Focus on maintaining a steady and controlled plucking technique.

Remember, developing a consistent and precise plucking motion takes time and dedicated practice. Be patient with yourself and maintain a focus on accuracy and control. By incorporating these tips into your practice routine, you will gradually improve your plucking technique and achieve greater mastery over the Jew's harp.

Chapter 3: Playing Techniques And Articulation

3.1 Single Note Melodies:

A. Step-By-Step Instructions To Play Melodies Using Single Notes

Playing melodies using single notes on the Jew's harp requires careful control and coordination. Here are step-by-step instructions to help you play melodies:

1. Familiarize Yourself with the Instrument:

- Take time to explore the Jew's harp and get a feel for its sound and responsiveness.
- Experiment with plucking the reed and familiarize yourself with the range of pitches it produces.

2. Choose a Simple Melody:

- Start with a simple melody that you are familiar with, such as a nursery rhyme or a folk tune.
- Select a melody that primarily consists of single notes, rather than complex intervals or chords.

3. Identify the Notes:

- Listen closely to the melody you want to play and identify the individual notes that make up the tune.
- Break down the melody into small sections or phrases, focusing on one phrase at a time.

4. Determine the Corresponding Notes on the Jew's Harp:

- Determine the pitch of each note in the melody and try to find the closest approximation on the Jew's harp.

- Experiment with different Jew's harps to find the one that best matches the desired range for your chosen melody.

5. Practice Playing Single Notes:

- Develop control over playing single notes on the Jew's harp by plucking the reed with your finger in a precise and controlled manner.
- Start by playing each note of the melody separately, focusing on accuracy and clarity.

6. Work on Timing and Rhythm:

- Pay attention to the timing and rhythm of the melody.
- Use a metronome or play along with a recorded version of the melody to ensure that you are playing in time.

7. Connect the Notes:

- Once you can play each note separately, work on connecting the notes to create a flowing melody.
- Smoothly transition from one note to the next, maintaining a consistent plucking technique and rhythm.

8. Add Expression and Dynamics:

- Experiment with adding dynamics and expression to the melody by varying the intensity and speed of your plucking.
- Explore techniques such as accenting certain notes, adding vibrato, or using slight variations in timing to bring the melody to life.

9. Practice, Practice, Practice:

- Dedicate regular practice sessions to playing melodies on the Jew's harp. Start slowly and gradually increase the tempo as you become more comfortable.

10. Experiment and Explore:

- Once you have mastered playing melodies using single notes, feel free to experiment with embellishments, variations, and improvisation.

- Explore different playing techniques, such as using tongue clicks or vocalizations, to add further depth and expressiveness to your melodies.

Remember, learning to play melodies on the Jew's harp takes time and patience. Break down the process into manageable steps and focus on accuracy and control. With practice and perseverance, you will be able to play a wide variety of melodies on the Jew's harp.

C. Practice Exercises To Improve Note Accuracy And Timing

Practicing specific exercises can help improve note accuracy and timing when playing melodies on the Jew's harp. Here are some exercises you can incorporate into your practice routine:

1. Isolated Note Practice:

- Choose a single note on the Jew's harp and play it repeatedly, focusing on accuracy and clarity.
- Ensure that each note is played with precision and consistency in terms of pitch and duration.
- Use a metronome or backing track to practice playing the note in time with a steady rhythm.

2. Note-to-Note Transitions:

- Select a simple two-note sequence from a melody and practice transitioning smoothly between the two notes.
- Start slowly, ensuring that each note is played accurately and that there are no pauses or hesitations between the transitions.
- Gradually increase the speed as you become more comfortable and confident with the transitions.

3. Scale Exercises:

- Play through different scales on the Jew's harp, focusing on maintaining accurate pitch and timing between each note.
- Start with a simple scale, such as a major or pentatonic scale, and practice ascending and descending smoothly.
- Pay attention to the intervals between each note, ensuring they are played with precision and consistency.

4. Rhythmic Patterns:

- Practice playing rhythmic patterns using single notes on the Jew's harp.
- Start with simple patterns, such as quarter notes or eighth notes, and gradually incorporate more complex rhythms.
- Use a metronome or backing track to maintain a steady tempo and improve your timing.

5. Melodic Phrase Repetition:

- Choose a short melodic phrase from a song or melody and repeat it multiple times.
- Focus on reproducing the phrase accurately each time, paying attention to both note accuracy and timing.
- Use a metronome or backing track to practice playing the phrase in time and develop a sense of rhythmic consistency.

6. Call and Response:

- Create a call-and-response exercise where you play a short melodic phrase and then repeat it back.

- This exercise helps improve your ability to mimic and reproduce melodic patterns accurately.

- Start with simple phrases and gradually increase the complexity as you become more proficient.

7. Record and Analyze:

- Record yourself playing melodies and listen back to identify areas where note accuracy and timing can be improved.

- Analyze any discrepancies or errors and focus on specific sections or notes that require more attention and practice.

8. Slow Practice and Gradual Tempo Increase:

- Begin practicing melodies at a slower tempo, ensuring accuracy and precision in note placement and timing.
- Gradually increase the tempo as you gain confidence and proficiency.
- Use a metronome to monitor your progress and maintain a consistent tempo.

Remember to approach these exercises with patience and consistency. Regular practice and focused attention on note accuracy and timing will help you develop greater control and precision when playing melodies on the Jew's harp.

3.2 Vibrato And Bending:

A. Adding Expressive Elements To Your Playing Through Vibrato And Bending Techniques

Adding expressive elements to your playing on the Jew's harp can greatly enhance the musicality and emotional depth of your performances. Two techniques commonly used for adding expression are vibrato and bending. Here's how you can incorporate these techniques into your playing:

1. Vibrato:

- Vibrato adds a pulsating or wavering effect to a sustained note, creating a sense of warmth and expressiveness.
- Start by playing a sustained note on the Jew's harp.

- Gradually vary the pressure of your finger on the reed while maintaining a consistent airflow.

- This slight modulation in pressure will cause the pitch of the note to fluctuate, creating a vibrato effect.

- Experiment with different speeds and widths of vibrato to find the desired expressive effect.

2. Bending:

- Bending involves altering the pitch of a note by manipulating your mouth shape or tongue position.

- Start by playing a sustained note on the Jew's harp.

- Experiment with slightly changing the shape of your mouth or the position of your tongue while maintaining the airflow.

- This manipulation will cause the pitch to bend either upwards (raising the pitch) or downwards (lowering the pitch).
- Practice bending the note gradually and smoothly, avoiding sudden or jerky movements.
- Combine bending with vibrato or incorporate it into melodic passages to add expressive nuances to your playing.

3. Controlled Dynamics:

- Dynamics refer to variations in volume and intensity in your playing.
- Experiment with playing certain notes or phrases softly (piano) and then gradually increasing the volume (crescendo) or vice versa.
- Use the strength and control of your finger plucking to achieve different dynamic levels.

- Combine dynamics with vibrato and bending techniques to create expressive and dynamic musical phrases.

4. Emotional Interpretation:

- Pay attention to the emotional character of the melody or the overall mood of the piece you are playing.
- Adjust your playing techniques, such as vibrato and bending, to convey the intended emotions.
- Experiment with different intensities, speeds, and combinations of vibrato and bending to match the emotional expression you desire.

5. Listen and Learn from Others:

- Listen to recordings of experienced Jew's harp players to gain inspiration and learn from their expressive techniques.

- Observe how they use vibrato, bending, and dynamics to convey emotions in their playing.
- Analyze their techniques and incorporate them into your own style and interpretation.

Remember to practice these expressive techniques gradually and with control. It may take time to develop the muscle memory and sensitivity required to execute them effectively. With consistent practice and experimentation, you will be able to add expressive elements like vibrato and bending to your Jew's harp playing, enriching your musical expression and captivating your audience.

B. Exercises To Develop Control And Range In Pitch Variation

Developing control and range in pitch variation is crucial for expressive playing on the Jew's harp. Here are some exercises to help you improve your control over pitch variations:

1. Pitch Slides:

- Start by playing a sustained note on the Jew's harp.
- Gradually slide the pitch up and down smoothly using subtle adjustments of your mouth shape, tongue position, or jaw movement.
- Practice sliding the pitch in both upward and downward directions, aiming for smooth and controlled transitions.

2. Interval Jumps:

- Choose a specific interval, such as a major second or perfect fifth.
- Play a sustained note and then jump to the target note of the chosen interval.
- Practice accurately hitting the target note with precision, avoiding any intermediary pitches.
- Gradually increase the difficulty by choosing larger intervals or more challenging jumps.

3. Microtonal Control:

- Experiment with producing microtonal variations by making subtle adjustments in your mouth shape or tongue position.
- Explore playing notes slightly higher or lower than the standard Western musical scale.

- Practice producing microtonal variations intentionally, focusing on accuracy and control over the subtle pitch changes.

4. Vibrato Exercises:

- As mentioned earlier, vibrato adds pitch variation to a sustained note.
- Practice different vibrato techniques, such as wide or narrow vibrato, slow or fast vibrato.
- Start with a sustained note and experiment with applying vibrato using variations in finger pressure and airflow.
- Focus on maintaining a consistent rhythm and control over the vibrato speed and width.

5. Bend and Release:

- Start with a sustained note on the Jew's harp.
- Gradually lower the pitch by manipulating your mouth shape or tongue position, creating a bend in the note.

- Hold the bent note for a moment and then release it back to the original pitch.
- Practice bending and releasing smoothly and accurately, without any sudden or jerky movements.

6. Melodic Exercises:

- Select a simple melodic phrase and focus on incorporating pitch variations within the melody.
- Experiment with using slides, bends, and microtonal variations to add expressive elements to the melodic lines.
- Practice playing the melodic phrases with control and precision, paying attention to the pitch variations.

7. Slow and Steady Practice:

- Start practicing these exercises at a slow tempo to ensure accuracy and control over the pitch variations.
- Gradually step up the speed as you gain more comfort and confidence.
- Use a metronome or backing track to maintain a steady tempo and practice in time.

8. Recording and Self-Evaluation:

- Record yourself practicing these exercises and listen back to evaluate the accuracy and quality of your pitch variations.
- Identify areas for improvement and focus on refining your control and range in pitch variation.

Chapter 4: Step By Step Instructions To Play 10 Song

It is essential to note that the Jew's harp can be used to play various melodies and songs across different genres. The listed songs below is just a starting point, as you can explore a wide range of musical styles, and adapt songs to suit the unique sound and characteristics of the Jew's harp.

1. "Oh! Susanna" by Stephen Foster

To play the song "Oh! Susanna" by Stephen Foster on the Jew's harp, follow these step-by-step instructions:

1. Familiarize yourself with the melody:
Listen to the song "Oh! Susanna" to get a good understanding of the melody and rhythm.

2. Identify the key: Determine the key of the song. "Oh! Susanna" is typically played in the key of C major.

3. Position the Jew's harp: Hold the Jew's harp firmly between your teeth with the frame resting against your lips.

4. Pluck the Jew's harp: Use your finger to pluck the tongue of the Jew's harp, producing a sound. Experiment with different finger placements and pressures to find the desired tone.

5. Play the first phrase: Begin by playing the first phrase of the melody. In "Oh! Susanna," it starts with the notes: C-C-C-E-G-G.

6. Practice the rhythm: Pay attention to the rhythm of the song. Maintain a steady beat and make sure your plucking motion aligns with the timing of the melody.

7. Continue with the rest of the song: Play through the entire song, following the melody and rhythm as closely as possible. The notes for the verses of "Oh! Susanna" are as follows:

Verse 1:

C-C-C-E-G-G

G-G-G-G-C-C

C-C-C-C-E-E

D-D-D-D-G-G

Chorus:

G-G-G-G-C-C

C-C-C-C-E-G

G-G-G-G-C-C

C-C-C-C-E-G

G-G-G-G-C-C

C-C-C-C-E-E

D-D-D-D-G-G

8. Practice and refine: Repeat the song multiple times, focusing on accuracy, timing, and smooth transitions between notes. Take your time to ensure that you are playing each note clearly and in tune.

9. Add variations and personal touches: Once you feel comfortable with the basic melody, experiment with adding variations, such as bends, vibrato, or rhythmic embellishments, to make the song your own.

2. "Jingle Bells" - James Lord Pierpont

To play the song "Jingle Bells" by James Lord Pierpont on the Jew's harp, follow these step-by-step instructions:

1. Familiarize yourself with the melody: Listen to the song "Jingle Bells" to become familiar with the melody and rhythm.

2. Identify the key: "Jingle Bells" is typically played in the key of G major.

3. Position the Jew's harp: Hold the Jew's harp firmly between your teeth with the frame resting against your lips.

4. Pluck the Jew's harp: Use your finger to pluck the tongue of the Jew's harp, producing a sound. Experiment with

different finger placements and pressures to find the desired tone.

5. Play the first phrase: Start by playing the first phrase of the melody. In "Jingle Bells," it begins with the notes: E-E-E-J-E-D.

6. Practice the rhythm: Pay attention to the rhythm of the song. Maintain a steady beat and ensure that your plucking motion aligns with the timing of the melody.

7. Continue with the rest of the song: Play through the entire song, following the melody and rhythm closely. The notes for the verses of "Jingle Bells" are as follows:

Verse 1:
E-E-E-J-E-D
E-E-E-J-E-D
E-G-C-D-E

F-F-E-E-E

Chorus:

G-G-G-G-G-E

G-G-G-G-G-E

G-G-A-A-G

F-F-E-E-E

8. Practice and refine: Repeat the song multiple times, focusing on accuracy, timing, and smooth transitions between notes. Ensure that you play each note clearly and in tune.

9. Add variations and personal touches: Once you feel comfortable with the basic melody, experiment with adding variations, such as bends, vibrato, or rhythmic embellishments, to make the song your own.

3. "Twinkle, Twinkle, Little Star" - Jane Taylor

To play the song "Twinkle, Twinkle, Little Star" by Jane Taylor on the Jew's harp, follow these step-by-step instructions:

1. Familiarize yourself with the melody: Listen to the song "Twinkle, Twinkle, Little Star" to become familiar with the melody and rhythm.

2. Identify the key: "Twinkle, Twinkle, Little Star" is typically played in the key of C major.

3. Position the Jew's harp: Hold the Jew's harp firmly between your teeth with the frame resting against your lips.

4. Pluck the Jew's harp: Use your finger to pluck the tongue of the Jew's harp, producing a sound. Experiment with different finger placements and pressures to find the desired tone.

5. Play the first phrase: Begin by playing the first phrase of the melody. In "Twinkle, Twinkle, Little Star," it starts with the notes: C-C-G-G-A-A.

6. Practice the rhythm: Pay attention to the rhythm of the song. Maintain a steady beat and ensure that your plucking motion aligns with the timing of the melody.

7. Continue with the rest of the song: Play through the entire song, following the melody and rhythm closely. The notes for the verses of "Twinkle, Twinkle, Little Star" are as follows:

Verse 1:

C-C-G-G-A-A

G-G-F-F-E-E

D-D-C-C-G-G

F-F-E-E-D-D

G-G-F-F-E-E

D-D-G-G-F-F

E-E-D-D-G-G

8. Practice and refine: Repeat the song multiple times, focusing on accuracy, timing, and smooth transitions between notes. Ensure that you play each note clearly and in tune.

9. Add variations and personal touches: Once you feel comfortable with the basic melody, experiment with adding variations, such as bends, vibrato, or rhythmic embellishments, to make the song your own.

4. "The Lion Sleeps Tonight" - The Tokens

To play the song "The Lion Sleeps Tonight" by The Tokens on the Jew's harp, follow these step-by-step instructions:

1. Familiarize yourself with the melody: Listen to the song "The Lion Sleeps Tonight" to become familiar with the melody and rhythm.

2. Identify the key: "The Lion Sleeps Tonight" is typically played in the key of C major.

3. Position the Jew's harp: Hold the Jew's harp firmly between your teeth with the frame resting against your lips.

4. Pluck the Jew's harp: Use your finger to pluck the tongue of the Jew's harp, producing a sound. Experiment with different finger placements and pressures to find the desired tone.

5. Play the first phrase: Start by playing the first phrase of the melody. In "The Lion Sleeps Tonight," it begins with the notes: C-E-G-G.

6. Practice the rhythm: Pay attention to the rhythm of the song. Maintain a steady beat and ensure that your plucking motion aligns with the timing of the melody.

7. Continue with the rest of the song: Play through the entire song, following the melody and rhythm closely. The notes for the verses of "The Lion Sleeps Tonight" are as follows:

Verse 1:

C-E-G-G

C-E-G-G

C-E-F-F

E-G-E-G

C-E-G-G

Chorus:

C-C-E-C-E-G-G

C-C-E-C-E-G-G

C-C-E-C-E-F-F

E-G-E-G

C-E-G-G

8. Practice and refine: Repeat the song multiple times, focusing on accuracy, timing, and smooth transitions between notes. Ensure that you play each note clearly and in tune.

9. Add variations and personal touches:

Once you feel comfortable with the basic melody, experiment with adding variations, such as bends, vibrato, or rhythmic embellishments, to make the song your own.

5. "House of the Rising Sun" - Traditional

To play the song "House of the Rising Sun" in a traditional style on the Jew's harp, follow these step-by-step instructions:

1. Familiarize yourself with the melody: Listen to the song "House of the Rising Sun" to become familiar with the melody and rhythm.

2. Identify the key: "House of the Rising Sun" is typically played in the key of Am (A minor).

3. Position the Jew's harp: Hold the Jew's harp firmly between your teeth with the frame resting against your lips.

4. Pluck the Jew's harp: Use your finger to pluck the tongue of the Jew's harp, producing a sound. Experiment with different finger placements and pressures to find the desired tone.

5. Play the first phrase: Start by playing the first phrase of the melody. In "House of the Rising Sun," it begins with the notes: E-E-C-A.

6. Practice the rhythm: Pay attention to the rhythm of the song. Maintain a steady beat and ensure that your plucking motion aligns with the timing of the melody.

7. Continue with the rest of the song: Play through the entire song, following the melody and rhythm closely. The notes for the verses of "House of the Rising Sun" are as follows:

Verse 1:

Am-C-D-F

Am-C-E-E

Am-C-D-F

Am-E-Am-E

Chorus:

C-E-Am-C

C-E-Am-C

C-E-Am-E

Am-E-Am-E

8. Practice and refine: Repeat the song multiple times, focusing on accuracy, timing, and smooth transitions between notes. Ensure that you play each note clearly and in tune.

9. Add variations and personal touches: Once you feel comfortable with the basic melody, experiment with adding variations,

such as bends, vibrato, or rhythmic
embellishments, to make the song your own.

6. "Amazing Grace" - John Newton

To play the song "Amazing Grace" by John Newton on the Jew's harp, follow these step-by-step instructions:

1. Familiarize yourself with the melody: Listen to the song "Amazing Grace" to become familiar with the melody and rhythm.

2. Identify the key: "Amazing Grace" is typically played in the key of G major.

3. Position the Jew's harp: Hold the Jew's harp firmly between your teeth with the frame resting against your lips.

4. Pluck the Jew's harp: Use your finger to pluck the tongue of the Jew's harp, producing a sound. Experiment with

different finger placements and pressures to find the desired tone.

5. Play the first phrase: Start by playing the first phrase of the melody. In "Amazing Grace," it begins with the notes: G-G-D-B.

6. Practice the rhythm: Pay attention to the rhythm of the song. Maintain a steady beat and ensure that your plucking motion aligns with the timing of the melody.

7. Continue with the rest of the song: Play through the entire song, following the melody and rhythm closely. The notes for the verses of "Amazing Grace" are as follows:

Verse 1:
G-G-D-B
G-G-E-C

D-D-B-G

C-C-A-G

Verse 2:

G-G-D-B

G-G-E-C

D-D-B-G

C-C-A-G

8. Practice and refine: Repeat the song multiple times, focusing on accuracy, timing, and smooth transitions between notes. Ensure that you play each note clearly and in tune.

9. Add variations and personal touches: Once you feel comfortable with the basic melody, experiment with adding variations, such as bends, vibrato, or rhythmic embellishments, to make the song your own.

7. "Scarborough Fair" - Traditional

To play the song "Scarborough Fair" in a traditional style on the Jew's harp, follow these step-by-step instructions:

1. Familiarize yourself with the melody: Listen to the song "Scarborough Fair" to become familiar with the melody and rhythm.

2. Identify the key: "Scarborough Fair" is typically played in the key of D minor.

3. Position the Jew's harp: Hold the Jew's harp firmly between your teeth with the frame resting against your lips.

4. Pluck the Jew's harp: Use your finger to pluck the tongue of the Jew's harp, producing a sound. Experiment with

different finger placements and pressures to find the desired tone.

5. Play the first phrase: Start by playing the first phrase of the melody. In "Scarborough Fair," it begins with the notes: D-A-D-G.

6. Practice the rhythm: Pay attention to the rhythm of the song. Maintain a steady beat and ensure that your plucking motion aligns with the timing of the melody.

7. Continue with the rest of the song: Play through the entire song, following the melody and rhythm closely. The notes for the verses of "Scarborough Fair" are as follows:

Verse 1:
D-A-D-G

D-A-D-C

D-A-Bb-A-G

D-A-D-G

Verse 2:

D-A-D-G

D-A-D-C

D-A-Bb-A-G

D-A-D-G

8. Practice and refine: Repeat the song multiple times, focusing on accuracy, timing, and smooth transitions between notes. Ensure that you play each note clearly and in tune.

9. Add variations and personal touches: Once you feel comfortable with the basic melody, experiment with adding variations, such as bends, vibrato, or rhythmic embellishments, to make the song your own.

8. "Greensleeves" - Traditional

To play the song "Greensleeves" in a traditional style on the Jew's harp, follow these step-by-step instructions:

1. Familiarize yourself with the melody: Listen to the song "Greensleeves" to become familiar with the melody and rhythm.

2. Identify the key: "Greensleeves" is typically played in the key of G major.

3. Position the Jew's harp: Hold the Jew's harp firmly between your teeth with the frame resting against your lips.

4. Pluck the Jew's harp: Use your finger to pluck the tongue of the Jew's harp, producing a sound. Experiment with

different finger placements and pressures to find the desired tone.

5. Play the first phrase: Start by playing the first phrase of the melody. In "Greensleeves," it begins with the notes: G-G-B-D.

6. Practice the rhythm: Pay attention to the rhythm of the song. Maintain a steady beat and ensure that your plucking motion aligns with the timing of the melody.

7. Continue with the rest of the song: Play through the entire song, following the melody and rhythm closely. The notes for the verses of "Greensleeves" are as follows:

Verse 1:
G-G-B-D
G-G-B-D

C-C-C-B

A-A-G

Verse 2:

G-G-B-D

G-G-B-D

C-C-C-B

A-A-G

8. Practice and refine: Repeat the song multiple times, focusing on accuracy, timing, and smooth transitions between notes. Ensure that you play each note clearly and in tune.

9. Add variations and personal touches: Once you feel comfortable with the basic melody, experiment with adding variations, such as bends, vibrato, or rhythmic embellishments, to make the song your own.

9. "Hava Nagila" - Traditional Jewish

To play the traditional Jewish song "Hava Nagila" on the Jew's harp, follow these step-by-step instructions:

1. Familiarize yourself with the melody: Listen to the song "Hava Nagila" to become familiar with the melody and rhythm.

2. Identify the key: "Hava Nagila" is typically played in the key of C major.

3. Position the Jew's harp: Hold the Jew's harp firmly between your teeth with the frame resting against your lips.

4. Pluck the Jew's harp: Use your finger to pluck the tongue of the Jew's harp, producing a sound. Experiment with

different finger placements and pressures to find the desired tone.

5. Play the first phrase: Start by playing the first phrase of the melody. In "Hava Nagila," it begins with the notes: C-C-D-E-E.

6. Practice the rhythm: Pay attention to the rhythm of the song. Maintain a steady beat and ensure that your plucking motion aligns with the timing of the melody.

7. Continue with the rest of the song: Play through the entire song, following the melody and rhythm closely. The notes for the verses of "Hava Nagila" are as follows:

Verse 1:
C-C-D-E-E
D-D-E-F-F
E-E-F-G-G

F-F-G-A-A

G-G-A-G-F-E-D-C

8. Practice and refine: Repeat the song multiple times, focusing on accuracy, timing, and smooth transitions between notes. Ensure that you play each note clearly and in tune.

9. Add variations and personal touches: Once you feel comfortable with the basic melody, experiment with adding variations, such as bends, vibrato, or rhythmic embellishments, to make the song your own.

10. "The Star-Spangled Banner" - Francis Scott Key

To play "The Star-Spangled Banner" by Francis Scott Key on the Jew's harp, follow these step-by-step instructions:

1. Familiarize yourself with the melody: Listen to a rendition of "The Star-Spangled Banner" to become familiar with the melody and rhythm.

2. Identify the key: "The Star-Spangled Banner" is typically played in the key of F major.

3. Position the Jew's harp: Hold the Jew's harp firmly between your teeth with the frame resting against your lips.

4. Pluck the Jew's harp: Use your finger to pluck the tongue of the Jew's harp, producing a sound. Experiment with different finger placements and pressures to find the desired tone.

5. Play the first phrase: Start by playing the first phrase of the melody. In "The Star-Spangled Banner," it begins with the notes: F-E-D-E-F.

6. Practice the rhythm: Pay attention to the rhythm of the song. Maintain a steady beat and ensure that your plucking motion aligns with the timing of the melody.

7. Continue with the rest of the song: Play through the entire song, following the melody and rhythm closely. The notes for the verses of "The Star-Spangled Banner" are as follows:

Verse 1:

F-E-D-E-F

G-G-F-E-D

F-E-D-E-F

E-E-F-G-A

G-F-E-D-E-F

8. Practice and refine: Repeat the song multiple times, focusing on accuracy, timing, and smooth transitions between notes. Ensure that you play each note clearly and in tune.

9. Add variations and personal touches: Once you feel comfortable with the basic melody, experiment with adding variations, such as bends, vibrato, or rhythmic embellishments, to make the song your own.

Chapter 5: Advanced Techniques And Styles

5.1 Overtones And Harmonics:

A. Exploring The World Of Overtones And Harmonics On The Jew's Harp

Exploring the world of overtones and harmonics on the Jew's harp can unlock a whole new dimension of sound and musical possibilities. Here are some tips to help you dive into this fascinating aspect of playing the Jew's harp:

1. Understand Overtones and Harmonics:

- Overtones are additional frequencies that are produced along with the fundamental frequency when a musical instrument is played.

- Harmonics refer to specific overtones that are related to the fundamental frequency through mathematical relationships.

2. Play with Mouth Shape and Position:

- Experiment with different mouth shapes and positions to explore different overtone and harmonic possibilities.
- Varying the shape and position of your mouth can emphasize or dampen specific overtones, creating different tonal qualities.

3. Control Your Breath:

- Manipulate your breath control to affect the strength and clarity of the overtones and harmonics.
- Experiment with different breathing techniques such as gentle exhalation or inhalation while playing to produce desired effects.

4. Explore Partial Dampening:

- Partially dampen the Jew's harp with your finger or thumb while playing to selectively suppress certain overtones.
- This technique allows you to create interesting and complex harmonic combinations by emphasizing or removing specific frequencies.

5. Experiment with Vibrations:

- Experiment with using your vocal cords or humming while playing the Jew's harp.
- The combination of the instrument's vibrations and vocal vibrations can create unique harmonic interactions.

6. Practice Mouth and Tongue Articulation:

- Develop control over your mouth and tongue articulation to manipulate overtones and harmonics.

- Try different tongue placements, articulation techniques, and movements to create various tonal effects.

7. Listen and Observe:
- Pay close attention to the sounds you produce while playing the Jew's harp.
- Observe how changes in mouth shape, breath control, and finger dampening affect the overtones and harmonics.
- Train your ears to identify different harmonic relationships and learn to recognize specific harmonics in your playing.

8. Experiment with Notations and Techniques:
- Explore different notations and techniques used to represent overtones and harmonics in music.

- Some musicians use specific symbols or notations to indicate the desired overtone or harmonic to play.

9. Transcribe and Analyze:

- Transcribe and analyze melodies or songs that heavily utilize overtones and harmonics.

- Study how the overtones and harmonics are employed to create specific musical effects and expressions.

B.Techniques To Produce Multiple Tones Simultaneously

Producing multiple tones simultaneously on the Jew's harp can create complex and harmonically rich sounds. Here are some techniques you can explore to achieve this effect:

1. Mouth Shape and Position:

- Experiment with different mouth shapes and positions to produce multiple tones simultaneously.
- Try shaping your mouth as if you're forming different vowel sounds to create separate resonating spaces.

2. Tongue Placement:

- Adjust the position of your tongue against the back of your teeth or palate to create additional tones.

- By altering the position of your tongue, you can create separate chambers for different tones to resonate.

3. Jaw Movement:
- Use slight jaw movements to create changes in tension and shape within your mouth.
- This can help you produce different pitches and harmonics simultaneously.

4. Vocalization:
- Combine vocalization with Jew's harp playing to produce multiple tones.
- Humming or vocalizing while playing can create harmonically rich textures and add depth to your sound.

5. Breath Control:
- Experiment with controlling your breath while playing the Jew's harp.

- Varying the intensity and speed of your breath can influence the pitch and timbre of the additional tones.

6. Partial Dampening:

- Use your finger or thumb to partially dampen specific parts of the Jew's harp while playing.
- This technique allows you to isolate certain reeds and create additional tones.

7. Overblowing:

- Explore overblowing techniques, similar to those used in wind instruments.
- By adjusting your breath pressure and angle, you can produce higher-pitched tones on the Jew's harp.

8. Combination of Techniques:

- Combine different techniques mentioned above to create complex and layered tones.

- Experiment with different combinations and find what works best for you in terms of producing multiple tones simultaneously.

9. Practice and Experiment:

- As with any skill, practice is essential to develop control and proficiency in producing multiple tones.
- Dedicate time to explore and experiment with these techniques, listening closely to the resulting sounds and making adjustments as needed.

Remember, producing multiple tones simultaneously on the Jew's harp requires patience, experimentation, and a keen ear.

5.2 Advanced Rhythms And Grooves:

A. Developing Rhythmic Patterns And Grooves Using The Jew's Harp

Developing rhythmic patterns and grooves on the Jew's harp can add a captivating and dynamic element to your playing. Here are some tips to help you develop rhythmic patterns and grooves using the Jew's harp:

1. Start with a Basic Rhythm:

- Begin by establishing a basic rhythmic pattern or groove.
- Choose a simple and steady rhythm as a foundation for your playing.

2. Focus on Timing and Consistency:

- Pay attention to your timing and strive for consistent and precise rhythmic execution.
- Practice with a metronome or drum track to develop a solid sense of timing.

3. Experiment with Different Note Durations:

- Vary the duration of the notes you play on the Jew's harp to create rhythmic interest.
- Combine shorter and longer notes to add rhythmic complexity to your patterns.

4. Incorporate Rests:

- Introduce rests or pauses between notes to create rhythmic accents and space.
- Rests can enhance the groove and give your playing a rhythmic "bounce."

5. Explore Syncopation:

- Experiment with syncopated rhythms by accenting off-beats or placing notes between the main beats.
- Syncopation can create an energetic and dynamic feel in your rhythmic patterns.

6. Layer Multiple Rhythmic Patterns:

- Develop the ability to layer multiple rhythmic patterns on top of each other.

- Practice playing different rhythms with different note durations simultaneously, creating polyrhythmic textures.

7. Use Articulation and Dynamics:

- Employ articulation techniques, such as tonguing or varying breath pressure, to shape the rhythmic patterns.

- Experiment with dynamics (volume changes) to add further expression and groove to your playing.

8. Draw Inspiration from Different Musical Styles:

- Listen to various musical genres and study the rhythmic patterns and grooves present in those styles.

- Draw inspiration from funk, jazz, world music, or any other genre that resonates with you and adapt their rhythmic elements to the Jew's harp.

9. Play Along with Backing Tracks or Metronomes:

- Use backing tracks or metronomes to practice playing your rhythmic patterns in time with a consistent beat.
- This will help you develop a strong sense of rhythm and improve your ability to lock in with other musicians.

10. Record and Listen:

- Record yourself playing your rhythmic patterns and grooves.
- Listen back to identify areas for improvement, evaluate the tightness of your rhythm, and refine your playing.

B.Syncopation And Polyrhythms For More Intricate Playing

Syncopation and polyrhythms can add intricacy and complexity to your Jew's harp playing. Here are some tips to help you incorporate syncopation and polyrhythms into your playing:

1. Understand Syncopation:

- Syncopation refers to emphasizing or accenting off-beats or weak beats within a rhythmic pattern.
- It creates tension and adds a unique rhythmic feel to the music.

2. Identify Strong and Weak Beats:

- Start by identifying the strong and weak beats in the rhythmic pattern you're working with.
- The strong beats are typically the downbeats (e.g., beats 1 and 3 in 4/4 time),

and the weak beats are the off-beats (e.g., beats 2 and 4 in 4/4 time).

3. Accent Off-Beats:

- Experiment with accenting the off-beats or weak beats in your rhythmic patterns.
- Play the Jew's harp slightly louder or with a more pronounced attack on those beats to create syncopation.

4. Subdivide the Beat:

- Divide each beat into smaller subdivisions to create intricate rhythmic patterns.
- Play shorter notes or use faster tongue movements within each beat to achieve subdivisions.

5. Overlapping Patterns:

- Layer multiple rhythmic patterns with different time signatures or note durations simultaneously.

- This creates polyrhythms, where different rhythms interlock and create complex rhythmic textures.

6. Practice with a Metronome:
- Use a metronome to develop a strong sense of timing and precision in your syncopated and polyrhythmic playing.
- Start slowly and gradually increase the tempo as you become more comfortable with the patterns.

7. Start Simple and Gradually Add Complexity:
- Begin by incorporating simple syncopated rhythms or polyrhythms into your playing.
- Once you feel comfortable, gradually introduce more intricate patterns and variations.

8. Listen and Internalize the Rhythmic Patterns:

- Listen to recordings of music that features syncopation and polyrhythms.
- Internalize the rhythmic patterns by tapping along, clapping, or counting out the beats.

9. Experiment with Different Articulation Techniques:

- Explore various articulation techniques on the Jew's harp, such as tongue placement, breath control, and jaw movement.
- Use these techniques to create subtle variations in note durations and emphasize syncopated or polyrhythmic elements.

10. Play Along with Music in Different Styles:

- Practice playing along with music in different genres that highlight syncopation and polyrhythms.
- Funk, Latin, African, and jazz music often feature intricate rhythmic patterns that can inspire your playing.

11. Improvise and Explore:

- Use improvisation as a way to explore syncopation and polyrhythms on the Jew's harp.
- Experiment with different combinations of rhythms, note durations, and accents to create your unique patterns.

Chapter 6: Performance And Stage Presence

6.1 Practice Strategies:

A. Effective Practice Routines To Enhance Your Skills

To enhance your skills on the Jew's harp, it's essential to establish effective practice routines. Here are some tips to help you structure your practice sessions:

1. Set Clear Goals:

- Clearly define what you want to achieve during each practice session.
- Set specific goals such as mastering a particular technique, improving rhythm, or learning a new song.

2. Warm-Up Exercises:

- Begin each practice session with warm-up exercises to prepare your body and mind for playing.
- Include exercises that focus on breath control, tongue articulation, and finger dexterity.

3. Technical Exercises:

- Dedicate time to practice specific techniques and skills.
- This may involve exercises that target hand placement, mouth positioning, plucking motion, or note accuracy.

4. Repertoire Practice:

- Spend time working on songs or melodies that you want to learn or improve.
- Break down complex passages into smaller sections and practice them gradually, focusing on precision and fluency.

5. Slow Practice:

- Practice challenging sections or techniques at a slower tempo to ensure accuracy and control.
- Gradually increase the speed as you gain proficiency, always maintaining a high level of accuracy.

6. Metronome Practice:

- Utilize a metronome to develop a solid sense of timing and rhythm.
- Practice playing along with the metronome, starting at a comfortable tempo and gradually increasing the speed.

7. Focus on Weak Areas:

- Identify your weaknesses and dedicate focused practice time to address them.
- Whether it's note accuracy, timing, or a specific technique, allocate sufficient time to work on these areas.

8. Experiment and Explore:

- It is essential to allocate a dedicated period for the purpose of engaging in creative exploration and experimentation.
- Try new techniques, improvisation, or adapting familiar songs to challenge yourself and broaden your musicality.

9. Record and Reflect:

- Record your practice sessions occasionally to objectively assess your progress.
- Listen back to identify areas that need improvement and celebrate your successes.

10. Take Breaks:

- Take short breaks during your practice session to rest your muscles and avoid strain.
- Use this time to reflect on your progress and mentally prepare for the next phase of practice.

11. Consistency:

- Aim for regular and consistent practice sessions rather than sporadic, lengthy sessions.
- Shorter, focused practices more frequently are often more effective in building skills than occasional long sessions.

B. Tips For Overcoming Common Challenges

Playing the Jew's harp can come with its own set of challenges. Here are some tips to help you overcome common difficulties and continue progressing in your playing:

1. Jaw Fatigue:

- If you experience jaw fatigue during extended playing sessions, take breaks and allow your jaw muscles to rest.
- Gradually increase your playing time over sessions to build endurance.
- Consider incorporating jaw stretching exercises to strengthen and relax the muscles.

2. Note Accuracy:

- Practice playing individual notes slowly and with precision.
- Use a tuner or recording device to check if you're hitting the desired pitch accurately.

- Focus on proper hand placement and consistent finger control.

3. Breath Control:
- Practice controlling your breath to achieve consistent and controlled sounds.
- Experiment with different levels of breath pressure to achieve different dynamics and tones.
- Take deep breaths and practice diaphragmatic breathing to increase breath support.

4. Tongue Placement and Articulation:
- Experiment with different tongue positions against the back of your teeth or palate to produce different sounds.
- Practice tongue articulation exercises, such as tongue slaps or trills, to improve dexterity and control.

- Focus on clear and precise articulation to produce distinct and crisp sounds.

5. Plucking Technique:
- Develop a consistent plucking motion using your finger.
- Practice plucking with a light and controlled touch, avoiding excessive force.
- Experiment with different finger positions and angles to find what works best for you.

6. Breath Noise:
- Minimize breath noise by focusing on breath control and maintaining a consistent airflow.
- Practice playing softly and gradually increase your volume while maintaining a clean sound.
- Experiment with different mouth shapes and angles to reduce unwanted breath noise.

7. Song Memorization:

- Break down songs into smaller sections and practice each section separately.
- Use repetition to memorize the sequences and patterns in the song.
- Practice playing without relying on written music or tabs to build your memorization skills.

8. Musical Interpretation:

- Listen to recordings of skilled Jew's harp players to gain inspiration and ideas for musical interpretation.
- Experiment with dynamics, phrasing, and articulation to add your personal touch to the music.
- Develop your ear by actively listening to the nuances and expressions in the music you're playing.

9. Patience and Persistence:

- Recognize that learning the Jew's harp takes time and patience.

- Embrace the learning process and enjoy the journey rather than solely focusing on the end result.

- Stay persistent and motivated, even during challenging times, and celebrate your progress along the way.

6.2 Performing With Confidence:

A. Techniques To Build Stage Presence And Connect With Your Audience

Building stage presence and connecting with your audience is crucial for a captivating and memorable performance on the Jew's harp. Here are some techniques to help you enhance your stage presence and establish a strong connection with your audience:

1. Confidence:

- Develop a sense of confidence in your playing and performance.
- Practice regularly to build your skills and knowledge of the instrument.
-Maintain confidence in your musical skills and have faith in your own abilities as a musician.

2. Body Language and Movement:

- Use your body language to convey the emotions and energy of the music.
- Stand tall with good posture, and be aware of your movements on stage.
- Incorporate subtle gestures, head nods, or body sways that align with the rhythm and dynamics of the music.

3. Eye Contact:

- Establish eye contact with individuals within the audience.
- Engage with individuals or sections of the audience, creating a personal connection.
- Avoid focusing solely on your instrument, and instead, let your eyes wander and connect with your listeners.

4. Facial Expressions:

- Use your facial expressions to convey the emotions and intensity of the music.

- Express joy, passion, concentration, or any other relevant emotions that the music evokes.
- Let your face show the connection you have with the music and the enjoyment of performing.

5. Interaction and Engagement:
- Interact with your audience through verbal communication or brief introductions to your songs.
- Encourage participation by inviting clapping, foot tapping, or other rhythmic responses.
- Show appreciation for your audience's presence and support.

6. Stage Movement:
- Utilize the stage space to your advantage.
- Move around the stage, but do so purposefully and with intention.

- Consider the dynamics of the music and use your movement to enhance the performance.

7. Emphasize Visual Appeal:

-Take time to think and plan carefully for your overall presentation.

- Dress appropriately for the performance and consider how your appearance aligns with the music and atmosphere you want to create.

- Use lighting effects or props that complement your performance and add visual interest.

8. Storytelling:

- Share anecdotes or stories related to the music or the Jew's harp.

- Provide context and background information to engage the audience on a deeper level.

- Connect the audience with the cultural and historical significance of the music you're playing.

9. Adapt to the Venue and Audience:
- Be mindful of the specific venue and the audience's expectations.
- Adjust your performance style, energy level, and song choices accordingly.
- Gauge the audience's reactions and adjust your performance to maintain their interest and connection.

10. Practice Performing:
- Practice performing in front of a mirror or record yourself to observe your stage presence.
- Seek opportunities to perform in front of others, such as open mic nights or small gatherings, to gain experience and confidence.

B.Advice On Overcoming Performance Anxiety

Performance anxiety is a common challenge that many musicians face, including those who play the Jew's harp. Here are some tips to help you overcome performance anxiety and perform with confidence:

1. Preparation:

- Thoroughly prepare your music and practice regularly to build confidence in your abilities.
- Rehearse performing in different settings, such as in front of friends or family, to simulate the performance experience.

2. Positive Self-Talk:

- Replace negative thoughts and self-doubt with positive affirmations.
- Remind yourself of your accomplishments and strengths as a musician.

3. Breathing Techniques:

- Practice deep breathing exercises to calm your nerves and center yourself before performing.
- Focus on slow, controlled breaths to regulate your heart rate and reduce tension.

4. Visualization:

- Visualize yourself performing successfully and confidently.
- Imagine the details of the performance, including the venue, the audience, and your own body language.

5. Gradual Exposure:

- Start performing in low-pressure environments, such as open mic nights or small gatherings, to gradually build your comfort level.

- Gradually increase the size of the audience and the complexity of the performance settings over time.

6. Focus on the Music:
- Shift your focus away from yourself and onto the music.
- Concentrate on the sounds you're producing and the emotional expression of the music, rather than worrying about judgment or mistakes.

7. Embrace Imperfections:
- Understand that making mistakes is a natural part of performing.
- Instead of dwelling on mistakes, focus on recovering and continuing to deliver a heartfelt performance.

8. Supportive Mindset:

- Remember that the audience is there to enjoy and appreciate the music.
- Imagine the audience as supportive and welcoming, rather than judgmental or critical.

9. Practice Performance:

- Simulate performance situations during your practice sessions.
- Perform in front of friends, family, or fellow musicians to gain experience and feedback.

10. Experience:

- The more you perform, the more comfortable and confident you'll become.
- Embrace opportunities to perform whenever possible, even if it feels challenging at first.

Printed in Dunstable, United Kingdom

77596248R00080